AWESOME HOCKEY TRIVIA FOR KIDS

Eric Zweig

illustrations by
Bill Dickson

Scholastic Canada Ltd.
Toronto New York London Auckland Sydney
Mexico City New Delhi Hong Kong Buenos Aires

To Amanda, like all of these books.
— Eric

Scholastic Canada Ltd.
604 King Street West, Toronto, Ontario M5V 1E1, Canada

Scholastic Inc.
557 Broadway, New York, NY 10012, USA

Scholastic Australia Pty Limited
PO Box 579, Gosford, NSW 2250, Australia

Scholastic New Zealand Limited
Private Bag 94407, Botany, Manukau 2163, New Zealand

Scholastic Children's Books
Euston House, 24 Eversholt Street, London NW1 1DB, UK

www.scholastic.ca

Library and Archives Canada Cataloguing in Publication
Title: Awesome hockey trivia for kids / Eric Zweig ; illustrations by Bill Dickson.
Names: Zweig, Eric, 1963- author. | Dickson, Bill, 1949- illustrator.
Identifiers: Canadiana 20220177163 | ISBN 9781443193870 (softcover)
Subjects: LCSH: National Hockey League—Miscellanea—Juvenile literature. |
LCSH: Hockey—Miscellanea—Juvenile literature. | LCGFT: Trivia and miscellanea.
Classification: LCC GV847.25 .Z937 2022 | DDC j796.962—dc23

CREDITS
Photos ©: cover, title page: Minas Panagiotakis/Getty Images; 23: Courtesy of the Jamaican
Olympic Ice Hockey Federation; 27: Paul Sancya/AP Photo; 64: mauritius images GmbH/
Alamy Stock Photo; 71: Mark Zaleski/AP Photo; 103: Dave Sandford/NHLI via Getty Images.

6 5 4 3 2 1   Printed in Canada 114   22 23 24 25 26

Introduction

In the introduction to *More Hockey Trivia for Kids*, I admitted that sometimes I worry about running out of stories to tell. That didn't seem to be a problem at all this time! In fact, there has been so much going on in hockey — and so many great players — in recent years that this book has a lot fewer old-time stories than these books usually do. For someone like me, who loves hockey history, that came as a bit of a surprise. At least I managed to get in something new about the strange old Stanley Cup series of 1905! That happened early in the previous century, but this book has even more weird and wonderful hockey happenings from more modern times. There are also a few stories about my all-time favourite player, Wayne Gretzky. With nearly 125 years of hockey history in this book, and plenty of stories about players you could watch on TV tonight, I hope you'll find a lot to like in these pages.

Longest. Season. Ever.

The 2019–20 NHL season began as usual on October 2, 2019. But, on March 12, 2020, the season was suspended indefinitely due to the COVID-19 pandemic. The NHL wouldn't resume play until August 1, 2020, with the last Stanley Cup Final game being held on September 28, nearly a full year after the season started.

Bubble Hockey

When play resumed on August 1, it would begin with the playoffs. Because not all teams had played the same number of games, the NHL expanded the playoffs from the usual 16 teams and four rounds of play to 24 teams and five rounds. Most unusual of all, because of COVID-19 travel restrictions, the teams were grouped in "bubbles" playing in two host cities. The teams in the NHL's Eastern Conference played their games in Toronto, and the Western Conference teams played in Edmonton. Both Conference Finals were held in Edmonton, then the Eastern Conference champions, the Tampa Bay Lightning, faced the Western Conference champions, the Dallas Stars, and Tampa won the Stanley Cup four games to two.

BY THE NUMBERS

For the first time ever, the 2019–20 playoffs were held in empty arenas, a measure intended to keep fans and players safe. Just how empty were those arenas? Toronto's Scotiabank Arena seats 18,800 and Rogers Place in Edmonton packs in 18,641. These are the five indoor arenas with the biggest capacity for NHL hockey games. The Canada Life Centre in Winnipeg, Manitoba home of the Jets is the smallest, seating 15,321.

ARENA	CITY	TEAM	CAPACITY
Bell Centre	Montreal	Canadiens	21,302
United Center	Chicago	Blackhawks	19,717
Wells Fargo Center	Philadelphia	Flyers	19,543
Little Caesars Arena	Detroit	Red Wings	19,515
Scotiabank Saddledome	Calgary	Flames	19,289

Oh, Canada

The late finish to the 2019–20 season, plus more concerns about the COVID-19 pandemic, meant the 2020–21 season had to be delayed. When it finally started on January 13, 2021, the season was limited to just 56 games.

There would be no bubbles this time, but because of pandemic travel restrictions limiting border crossings between Canada and the United States, the 2020–21 NHL season featured a new alignment of the league's divisions. Instead of Metropolitan, Atlantic, Central and Pacific, there was North, East, West and Central. The North Division was made up of the NHL's seven Canadian teams: the Montreal Canadiens, the Ottawa Senators, the Toronto Maple Leafs, the Winnipeg Jets, the Calgary Flames, the Edmonton Oilers and the Vancouver Canucks.

This was the first all-Canadian division since the NHL's first seven seasons, from 1917–18 through 1923–24, when the league only had Canadian teams and didn't have separate divisions. (There were only three and four teams in the entire NHL during those years!)

From 1926–27 through 1937–38, the NHL had between eight and ten teams and was split into two divisions known as the Canadian and the American. But in addition to teams from Toronto, Montreal and Ottawa, the Canadian Division also included a team called the New York Americans, so it wasn't actually all-Canadian at all!

Did You Know?

The teams that played in the very first NHL season were the Montreal Wanderers, the Montreal Canadiens, the Toronto Arenas and the Ottawa Senators. But the Wanderers withdrew from the NHL after a fire destroyed their arena on January 2, 1918.

BY THE NUMBERS

A 56-game season is pretty short by modern NHL standards, but there have been even shorter seasons too. The 2004–05 season was cancelled completely because of a lockout, with zero games played. In 1994–95 and 2012–13, teams played only 48 games each after nearly half of those seasons were wiped out by labour disruptions. The shortest season in NHL history was only 18 games long, back in 1918–19, when there were only three teams in the NHL. Here's how the NHL schedule has grown and changed over the years.

SEASON(S)	GAMES	TEAMS
1917–18	22	3 to 4
1918–19	18	3
1919–20 to 1923–24	24	4
1924–25	30	6
1925–26	36	7
1926–27 to 1930–31	44	10
1931–32 to 1941–42	48	7 to 9
1942–43 to 1945–46	50	6
1946–47 to 1948–49	60	6
1949–50 to 1966–67	70	6
1967–68	74	12
1968–69 to 1969–70	76	12
1970–71 to 1973–74	78	14 to 16
1974–75 to 1991–92	80	17 to 22
1992–93 to 1993–94	84	24 to 26
1994–95	48*	26
1995–96 to 2011–12	82	26 to 30
2012–13	48*	30
2013–14 to 2018–19	82	30 to 31
2019–20	68 to 71**	31
2020–21	56**	31
2021–22	82	32

*season affected by lockout   **season affected by the COVID-19 pandemic

Poulin Power

Big goals in big games are nothing new for Marie-Philip Poulin. She began representing Canada on the international stage when she was only 16 years old. She played in her first Women's World Championship in 2009. That tournament began just after her 18th birthday, making her the youngest woman on the team.

Poulin was still 18 years old and the youngest player when she scored both goals in Canada's 2–0 gold medal win over the United States at the 2010 Vancouver Olympics. Then, in the 2014 Sochi Games final against the U.S., Canada was trailing 2–1 until Poulin got the tying goal with just 55 seconds left in the third period. She then scored a big goal at 8:10 of overtime to get Canada the gold.

Poulin was the hero again at the 2022 Beijing Olympics. She scored in the first and second periods of the gold medal game, and her second goal proved to be the game-winner in a 3–2 Canadian victory against the U.S.

Hockey Loves Soccer

When the Canadian National Women's Hockey Team was in Calgary practising for the upcoming 2021 World Championships, they all got up early to watch the Canadian National Women's Soccer Team defeat Sweden for the gold medal at the Tokyo Summer Olympics. "We wanted to get on the ice right after that game," said Marie-Philip Poulin, captain of the women's hockey team. "We were all fired up!"

Just like their soccer compatriots, the Canadian National Women's Hockey Team made it to the gold medal game which ended regulation time in a tie, but scored in overtime for the big win.

Worth the Wait!

The members of the Canadian National Women's Hockey Team had barely played since the 2019 World Championship. The pandemic had wiped out the 2020 tournament and forced the 2021 event to be postponed from its usual start in April all the way until August.

Canada had once dominated the Women's World Championship, beating the United States in the gold-medal game nine times from 1990 until 2007. But since 2008, Canada had won the tournament only once! The United States had won five times in a row heading into the 2021 World Championship.

Things didn't look good at the start, when Canada fell behind Finland 2−0 in the first period of their very first game, but they rallied for a 5−3 victory. Next came a 5−1 win over Russia, followed by a 5−0 win over Switzerland. The biggest victory was a 5−1 win over the United States to close out the opening round.

In the playoffs, Canada dumped Germany
7–0 in the quarter-finals, then defeated
Switzerland again, this time 4–0, in the
semifinals. It was on to the finals now, where
their opponents would once again be their
archrivals from the United States.

The U.S.'s Alex Carpenter scored twice in
the first 20 minutes of the gold-medal game to
take a 2–0 lead. In the second period, Brianne
Jenner and Jamie Lee Rattray tied things
up with two quick goals. After that, there
was no more scoring right through the end
of the third. Then in OT, Brianne Jenner set
up Marie-Philip Poulin for a bullet drive that
went off the crossbar and into the net, giving
Canada their first championship in nine years!

Champa Bay

On October 17, 2020 — less than three weeks after the Tampa Bay Lightning won the Stanley Cup — baseball's Tampa Bay Rays became champions of the American League. Then on February 7, 2021, the Tampa Bay Buccaneers of the National Football League won the Super Bowl. And then exactly five months later, on July 7, 2021, the Lightning won the Stanley Cup for the second year in a row!

MASCOT MAYHEM

ThunderBug, a yellow and black lightning bug, is the mascot of the Tampa Bay Lightning. He wears number 00 and beats on a bass drum (it sounds like thunder) to accompany the song "Thunderstruck" by AC/DC before games.

Lucky Charm?

When the Washington Capitals won the Stanley Cup in 2018, it was the first for the team since joining the NHL in 1974. As part of their celebrations, the Caps took the Cup to a Washington Nationals baseball game.

The following season, Capitals superstar Alex Ovechkin threw out the first pitch in game four of the National League Division Series, sparking a winning streak that took the Nationals all the way to clinching the World Series. Like the Caps, it was the first-ever championship for the Nats.

Then at the November 3, 2019, Caps game, players from the two teams sang "We Are The Champions" together in the dressing room before the Nats were honoured at center ice prior to the opening faceoff. But the fan highlight of the evening came during the second intermission when six Nationals players paraded their trophy around the rink on the Zamboni machine.

BY THE NUMBERS

Since the 1985–86 season, the NHL has awarded the Presidents' Trophy to the team that finishes first overall in the regular-season standings. These eight teams have won the Presidents' Trophy and the Stanley Cup in the same year:

YEAR	TEAM	SEASON RECORD*	POINTS
1987	Edmonton Oilers	50-24-6	106
1989	Calgary Flames	54-17-9	117
1994	New York Rangers	52-24-8	112
1999	Dallas Stars	51-19-12	114
2001	Colorado Avalanche	52-16-10-4	118
2002	Detroit Red Wings	51-17-10-4	116
2008	Detroit Red Wings	54-21-7	115
2013	Chicago Blackhawks	36-7-5	77

*records are Win-Loss-Tie from 1986 to 1999, Win-Loss-Tie-Overtime Loss from 2000 to 2004 and Win-Loss-Overtime Loss from 2006 to present

But these seven teams were eliminated in the first round of the playoffs the same year they won the Presidents' Trophy!

YEAR	TEAM	SEASON RECORD*	POINTS
1991	Chicago Blackhawks	49-23-8	106
2000	St. Louis Blues	51-19-11-1	114
2006	Detroit Red Wings	58-16-8	124
2009	San Jose Sharks	53-18-11	117
2010	Washington Capitals	54-15-13	121
2012	Vancouver Canucks	51-22-9	111
2019	Tampa Bay Lightning	62-16-4	128

*records are Win-Loss-Tie from 1986 to 1999, Win-Loss-Tie-Overtime Loss from 2000 to 2004 and Win-Loss-Overtime Loss from 2006 to present

Hardware Hat Tricks

Pat Maroon of Tampa Bay not only won the Stanley Cup in back-to-back seasons with the Lightning in 2020 and 2021, but also played with the St. Louis Blues when they won the Cup in 2019, giving him three championships in a row.

Luke Schenn was also a two-time winner with Tampa Bay, giving his family three straight Stanley Cup titles after his brother, Brayden Schenn, won with St. Louis in 2019.

Trophy Tales

Many NHL players believe it's bad luck to touch the Stanley Cup if you haven't won it yet. It could mean they'll never win it. When St. Louis Blues center Brayden Schenn got his day with the Cup and brought it home to Saskatoon in the summer of 2019, there was a huge party. When Brayden's older brother Luke, who plays for the Tampa Bay Lightning, was invited to drink from the Cup, he got creative. "I drank out of it with a straw," he explained, "that doesn't count as touching it." The straw must have worked. The following season Luke went on to win the Cup he took pains not to touch.

Picture Perfect

When future NHL star Corey Perry was eight years old, he attended a hockey school in Rouyn-Noranda, Quebec. It was 1993 and Eric Desjardins, who was from Rouyn, had just won the Stanley Cup with the Montreal Canadiens. Desjardins brought the trophy to the hockey school, and Perry got his picture taken with it. The next time Perry got his picture taken with the Stanley Cup was 14 years later, in 2007, when he won it in his second season in the NHL, with the Anaheim Ducks. It would be another 13 years before Perry played for the Stanley Cup again. That time, as a member of the Dallas Stars, he lost the 2020 Final to Tampa Bay. In 2021, Perry lost the Cup to Tampa Bay again, this time as a member of the Montreal Canadiens. No wonder that Perry signed with the Lightning the 2021–22 season.

James Norris Trophy winner Victor Hedman also smiled for the camera with the Stanley Cup as a kid and an adult. Six-year-old Hedman got his picture taken with the

Stanley Cup in his hometown of Ornskoldsvik, Sweden, when Peter Forsberg got his day to bring the Stanley Cup home after winning it with the Colorado Avalanche in 1996. Hedman went on to win the Stanley Cup with Tampa Bay twice, in 2020 and 2021. On September 4, 2021, he got to bring the Stanley Cup home to Ornskoldsvik too.

Did You Know?

Ulf Sterner became the first player from Sweden to play in an NHL game when he stepped on the ice for the New York Rangers on January 27, 1965.

Kids these Days

Robert Thomas went from winning the championship of the Ontario Hockey League as an 18-year-old junior with the Hamilton Bulldogs in 2018 to winning the Stanley Cup as a 19-year-old rookie with the St. Louis Blues in 2019.

During the Blues' second-round win over the Dallas Stars that spring, Thomas set up Pat Maroon for the series-winning goal in a 2–1 overtime victory in game seven. At age 19, he became the second-youngest player in NHL history to figure in a series-clinching overtime goal. The only player younger than Thomas was Bep Guidolin of the Boston Bruins. Guidolin was the youngest player in NHL history when he began the 1942–43 season at just 16 years and 11 months old. He was 17 years old when he set up Ab DeMarco for the overtime winner that eliminated Montreal in the first round of the 1943 playoffs.

Gimme Five

On March 5, 2020, Mika Zibanejad scored five goals in a 6−5 win over the Washington Capitals, joining Don Murdoch (October 12, 1976) and Mark Pavelich (February 23, 1983) as the only players in New York Rangers history to score five goals in a single game. He was the first player in the NHL to score five goals since Patrik Laine did it for Winnipeg against St. Louis on November 24, 2018, and just the second player in NHL history to score his fifth goal of a game in overtime. The only player to do that before Zibanejad was Hall of Famer Sergei Fedorov of the Detroit Red Wings, against the Washington Capitals on December 26, 1996.

Hockey Is Hot!

Hockey is becoming popular in some unexpected places — like Latin America. The Amerigol LATAM Cup grew out of a previous competition known as the Pan American Ice Hockey Tournament, which was held from 2014 through 2017.

The Amerigol LATAM Cup has been held in the southern U.S. since 2018, although the 2020 tournament was cancelled due to the COVID-19 pandemic. The event returned bigger than ever in 2021 with 29 teams from 19 countries. They competed in five different divisions: two men's groups, a women's competition and two youth divisions. There were teams from Mexico, Puerto Rico, Venezuela, Argentina, Brazil, Chile and Colombia. There were also combined teams representing other Central American, South American and Caribbean countries. Colombia brought 80 players to the 2021 tournament, more than any other country, and beat Puerto Rico to win the top men's division.

Jamaica won the LATAM Cup at the 2019 tournament and was considered so strong compared to the rest of the competition that they only played exhibition games at the 2021 LATAM Cup.

The Jamaican team hopes to compete in the 2026 Winter Olympics in Italy.

Hockey Night in Puerto Rico

On September 23, 2006, the New York Rangers met the Florida Panthers in an NHL exhibition game played in San Juan, Puerto Rico. It was the first NHL game ever played in the Caribbean.

The game came a year after the grand opening of the 18,500-seat Jose Miguel Agrelot Coliseum, but only about 5,000 fans showed up to see the Rangers score a 3–2 victory.

The territory is not yet a member of the International Ice Hockey Federation, but the Puerto Rican National Men's Team made its debut in 2019 at the Amerigol LATAM Cup in South Florida. At the 2021 tournament, it had teams in the men's first division and the men's second division. Puerto Rico also entered its first National Women's Team and won the women's event!

NAME GAME: Team Names

The kraken is a mythical and mighty sea creature often depicted as a giant squid. Seattle is a port city on the Pacific Ocean with a long maritime history. The Seattle Kraken reflected this history in their team colours, which are described as deep sea blue, ice blue, shadow blue, boundless blue and red alert.

Getting Gritty

When the Flyers welcomed the Kraken on their first visit to Philadelphia on October 18, 2021, popular hometown mascot Gritty had a little bit of fun with the fact that the new Seattle team didn't have a mascot yet. Gritty unveiled his own creation — Cuddles the Kraken, who was just a man in a poorly made octopus costume. Philly fans booed . . . until Gritty gave Cuddles a pie in the face.

On March 5, 2022, Gritty continued making news when he appeared on a variant front cover of Marvel's *The Avengers* 53, alongside Iron Man. Five thousand fans who attended the game that day got a free copy of the limited-edition comic. Gritty, dressed as Thanos, inspired the Philadelphia Flyers to a 4–3 victory over the Chicago Blackhawks.

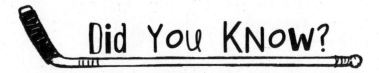

Did You Know?

When Auston Matthews won the Rocket Richard Trophy for leading the NHL in goals for the 2020–21 season (41 goals in 52 games played), he was the first member of the Toronto Maple Leafs to lead the NHL in goals in 75 years. The last to do it was Gaye Stewart back in 1945–46.

Auston Matthews was picked first overall by the Leafs in the 2016 NHL Draft.

BY THE NUMBERS

Only three players in NHL history have led the playoffs in scoring with 30 points or more in two or more consecutive seasons. One of them did it twice.

PLAYER, TEAM	YEAR	POINTS	GOALS	ASSISTS	GAMES
Wayne Gretzky, Edmonton	1983	38	12	26	16
Wayne Gretzky, Edmonton	1984	35	13	22	19
Wayne Gretzky, Edmonton	1985	47	17	30	18
Wayne Gretzky, Edmonton	1987	34	5	29	21
Wayne Gretzky, Edmonton	1988	43	12	31	19
Mario Lemieux, Pittsburgh	1991	44	16	28	23
Mario Lemieux, Pittsburgh	1992	34	16	18	15
Nikita Kucherov, Tampa Bay	2020	34	7	27	25
Nikita Kucherov, Tampa Bay	2021	32	8	24	23

NAME GAME:
Team Names

About 300 kilometres (180 mi) apart on the northern shore of Lake Huron, the Ontario towns of Sudbury and Sault Ste. Marie have been hockey rivals for more than 100 years. During the 1919–20 season, Sudbury fans had begun referring to their team as the "Wolves of the North." By the next season, the Sault Ste. Marie coach suggested the name Greyhounds for his team because "a greyhound is much faster than a wolf." Both the Wolves and the Greyhounds joined the Northern Ontario Hockey Association in 1962 and entered the OHL in 1972. Good dogs!

Did You Know!

When Wayne Gretzky joined the Greyhounds in 1977, he wanted to wear number 9 for his idol Gordie Howe, but it was already taken. Gretzky then chose number 14. After a few games, coach Muzz MacPherson suggested number 99, because two nines would be better than one.

BY THE NUMBERS

On February 17, 2021, Edmonton Oilers superstar Connor McDavid set up a goal by Jesse Puljujarvi at 3:45 of the first period of a game against the Winnipeg Jets. It was the 500th point of McDavid's career in just his 369th game. At 24 years old, McDavid became the 21st player in NHL history to reach 500 points before he turned 25. The only other active players to have done so are Sidney Crosby (in his 369th game) and Alex Ovechkin (in his 373rd game). Here are the 10 NHL players who reached 500 points in the fewest games:

PLAYER	GAMES
Wayne Gretzky	234
Mario Lemieux	287
Peter Stastny	322
Mike Bossy	349
Eric Lindros	352
Jari Kurri	356
Bryan Trottier	362
Sidney Crosby	369
Connor McDavid	369
Kent Nilsson	372

Trophy Tales

The Kelly Cup has been handed out to the champions of the ECHL since 1997. The official name of the trophy is the Patrick J. Kelly Cup, and it's named after the man who served as the league's first commissioner, from the 1988–89 season through the 1995–96 season.

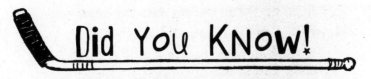

Did You Know!

On June 4, 2019, the Newfoundland Growlers beat the Toledo Walleye 4–3 to win the Kelly Cup as champions of the ECHL. With this victory, the farm team of the Toronto Maple Leafs became the first team from Newfoundland to win a professional sports championship.

NAME GAME:
Team Names

The Newfoundland Growlers began playing in the ECHL for the 2018–19 season and became champions in their first go-round!

Before the team name was announced on May 22, 2018, several others had been under consideration. They included the Shamrocks, the Storm and the Regiment. Growler actually has two meanings, one being the sound of a fierce animal and the other being a term for a small piece of an iceberg, which can often be seen floating past the coast of Newfoundland and Labrador.

The Growlers' colours are gold and black, and on their sweaters is the gruff face of a large Newfoundland dog. It's not just any dog. The Growlers' dog is inspired by the mascot of the Royal Newfoundland Regiment that served in World War I. His name was Sable Chief. He was a huge dog that weighed about 68 kilograms (150 lb.) and became well known for his immense size and dignified demeanour.

Dallas Cowboys?

Toward the end of the 2018–19 season, Dallas Stars Foundation president Marty Turco (who was a goalie with the team from 2000 to 2010) announced a partnership with a Texas cattle company that made the Stars the first NHL team to adopt a cow as their official team pet. Fans were given the chance to name the cow in a poll that included names based on former Stars players:

- Mike Moodano (for Mike Modano)
- Andy Moooooog (for Andy Moog)
- Sergei Moobov (for Sergei Zubov)
- Joe Mooendyk (for Joe Nieuwendyk)

The winning name was Mike Moodano — a pretty good choice, since Mike Modano is the all-time franchise leader in games played (1,459), goals (557), assists (802) and points (1359).

NAME GAME:
Classic Nicknames

Wayne Gretzky became a national celebrity during the winter of 1971–72, when he turned 11 years old. That year, playing for the Nadrofsky Steelers in his hometown of Brantford, Ontario, Gretzky scored 378 goals and had 139 assists for 517 points in 85 games played. Headlines referring to him as "Gretzky the Great" began appearing in Canadian newspapers at the end of that season. By the time he was playing junior hockey with the Sault Ste. Marie Greyhounds as a 16-year-old in 1977–78, newspapers were calling him "The Great Gretzky." American newspapers picked up on that nickname after 17-year-old Gretzky signed his first professional contract with the Indianapolis Racers of the World Hockey Association (WHA) on June 12, 1978. One of the earliest references to Gretzky as "the Great One" appears in a headline in *The Globe and Mail* newspaper on March 30, 1981, near the end of his second season in the NHL. With more than 60 NHL records set during his 20-year career from 1979 until 1999, it's no wonder that Gretzky remains the Great One.

Point Man

The NHL's regular season in 2020–21 was limited to just 56 games, but Connor McDavid still managed to score an amazing 105 points (33 goals, 72 assists). McDavid's teammate Leon Draisaitl finished a distant second with 84 points, while no one else even cracked 70. If McDavid had been able to score at the same pace over a regular 82-game season, he would have scored 154 points and joined Wayne Gretzky, Mario Lemieux, Steve Yzerman and Phil Esposito as the only players to top 150.

Did You Know?

When Tampa Bay's Nikita Kucherov won the Art Ross Trophy as the NHL's scoring leader in 2018–19, his 128 points that year (41 goals, 87 assists) were the most in the NHL since Mario Lemieux led the league with 161 points in 1995–96.

BY THE NUMBERS

If the 2020–21 season hadn't been shortened, Connor McDavid could have hit 154 points. These are the only players to score more than that in a season:

PLAYER	TEAM
Wayne Gretzky	Edmonton Oilers
Wayne Gretzky	Edmonton Oilers
Wayne Gretzky	Edmonton Oilers
Wayne Gretzky	Edmonton Oilers
Mario Lemieux	Pittsburgh Penguins
Wayne Gretzky	Edmonton Oilers
Wayne Gretzky	Edmonton Oilers
Mario Lemieux	Pittsburgh Penguins
Wayne Gretzky	Los Angeles Kings
Wayne Gretzky	Edmonton Oilers
Wayne Gretzky	Los Angeles Kings
Mario Lemieux	Pittsburgh Penguins
Mario Lemieux	Pittsburgh Penguins
Steve Yzerman	Detroit Red Wings

SEASON	GP	G	A	PTS
1985–86	80	52	163	215
1981–82	80	92	120	212
1984–85	80	73	135	208
1983–84	74	87	118	205
1988–89	76	85	114	199
1982–83	80	71	125	196
1986–87	79	62	121	183
1987–88	77	70	98	168
1988–89	78	54	114	168
1980–81	80	55	109	164
1990–91	78	41	122	163
1995–96	70	69	92	161
1992–93	60	69	91	160
1988–89	80	65	90	155

He's Got Hart

Not surprisingly, Connor McDavid won the Hart Trophy as NHL MVP for the 2020–21 season. McDavid received first-place votes on all 100 ballots cast, making him only the second unanimous winner of the Hart Trophy since it was first presented all the way back in 1924. The only other unanimous winner was Wayne Gretzky in 1981–82.

Going After Gretzky

During his 21 years playing professional hockey in the NHL and the World Hockey Association, Gretzky collected 3,369 points in the regular season and the playoffs combined. That's so many that a person could play hockey almost their whole life and never match it.

But Ken White, of Sexsmith, Alberta, came close. Born on March 24, 1944, Ken played as a high-level amateur until he was 40, then played recreational hockey for almost another 40 years. When he wasn't on the ice, Ken worked in radio and often called the play-by-play for recreational hockey games.

Ken loved hockey cards as a kid, especially the statistics. So he carefully kept track of his own stats. In 2000 he decided to see if he could catch the Great One!

"It's considered bad form to count your points in old-timers hockey," says Ken, "so I didn't tell any teammates and only shared this 'chase' with a few close friends."

By the spring of 2021 — right around his 77th birthday — Ken was up to 3,185 points. Unfortunately, he dislocated a hip while playing. He was only 184 points from Gretzky's record and figured that if he could play 60 games a year for the next two years, he could catch him. Still, with his injury, Ken decided it was time to slow down.

"I don't know if Gretzky's [more] relieved or if my wife is [more] relieved," he joked, "but it was fun while it lasted."

What a Guy(le)!

Professional players who topped 2,000 points in their entire careers (regular season and playoffs combined) include superstars Wayne Gretzky, Gordie Howe, Mark Messier, Jaromir Jagr and . . . Guyle Fielder?

Fielder came right out of junior hockey to play three games with the Chicago Black Hawks during the 1950–51 season. His last NHL games were with the Detroit Red Wings in the 1957–58 season, but in his total of 15 NHL games, Fielder had no goals and no assists. Yet from 1951–52 through the 1972–73 season, Fielder starred for 22 years in the minors, mostly in the Western Hockey League, but he also played for a time in the American Hockey League and the Pacific Coast Hockey League. Fielder won nine WHL scoring titles and six MVP awards, accumulating 2,037 points during his minor-league career. Fielder is the only professional player in hockey history to top 2,000 points in his career without ever scoring a single point in the NHL.

IIII IIII IIII IIII IIII IIII IIII IIII IIII IIII
IIII IIII IIII IIII IIII IIII IIII IIII IIII IIII
IIII IIII IIII IIII IIII IIII IIII IIII IIII IIII
IIII IIII IIII IIII IIII IIII IIII IIII IIII IIII

Games On

On April 19, 2021, Patrick Marleau of the San Jose Sharks suited up for his 1,768th game to set a new all-time record for games played, breaking the record Gordie Howe had kept for more than 40 years.

Marleau's career began in 1997–98, after San Jose took him as the second pick in the 1997 Entry Draft. When Marleau made his NHL debut on October 1, 1997, he was just 16 days past his 18th birthday. That made him the youngest player to start his NHL career since 1945.

IIII IIII IIII IIII IIII IIII IIII IIII IIII IIII
IIII IIII IIII IIII IIII IIII IIII IIII IIII IIII
IIII IIII IIII IIII IIII IIII IIII IIII IIII IIII

Keeping It in the Family

When Josh Anderson was traded from the Columbus Blue Jackets to the Montreal Canadiens in 2020, it was a dream come true. Josh was born and raised in Burlington, Ontario, which is usually Toronto Maple Leafs territory. Even so, Josh grew up cheering for the Canadiens. His father was from Montreal and had followed the team in the 1960s and '70s when they were winning tons of Stanley Cup titles. Josh's mother is a niece of Peter Mahovlich, who was a Canadiens star in the 1970s. The team was a family tradition.

On Josh's 16th birthday, in 2010, his dad got him tickets for a Canadiens playoff game in Montreal. Josh had dreams of making it to the NHL, and the atmosphere at that game fuelled the fire. Wonder what he wished for when he blew out his birthday candles . . .

MASCOT MAYHEM

S.J. Sharkie is the mascot of the San Jose
Sharks. He was introduced in 1992, partway
through the Sharks' inaugural NHL season.
Sharkie made the highlight reel after
a game on March 12, 1999. During
the pre-game festivities he was
rappelling down from the rafters
when, 12 metres (40 ft.) above
the ice, he became stuck
in the rope. Poor Sharkie
hung there until rescue
crews got him down.
Thankfully he was
fine — and so were
the Sharks, who
defeated the Detroit
Red Wings 2–0.

BY THE NUMBERS

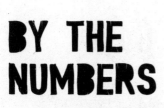

Only four players in hockey history have scored 100 points in each of their first three NHL seasons. All four did it during the high-flying 1980s.

PLAYER	SEASONS	POINTS
Wayne Gretzky	1979–80	137
	1980–81	164
	1981–82	212
Mike Rogers	1979–80	105
	1980–81	105
	1981–82	103
Peter Stastny	1980–81	109
	1981–82	139
	1982–83	124
Mario Lemieux	1984–85	100
	1985–86	141
	1986–87	107

Disco Guy!

The Montreal Canadiens are older than the NHL. Since they formed in 1909–10, the Canadiens have won the Stanley Cup 24 times, more than any other team by far. The Canadiens have also boasted some of the biggest stars in the game. Players such as Howie Morenz, Maurice Richard and Jean Beliveau are all legends . . . but only one Montreal hockey star moved to a disco beat!

Guy Lafleur was the NHL's biggest star of the 1970s. For six straight seasons, from 1974–75 through 1979–80, Lafleur had at least 50 goals and 100 points every year — and he led Montreal to the Stanley Cup four years in a row, from 1976 through 1979. In 1979, Lafleur came out with an instructional hockey album called *Lafleur!*, which was set to disco music. On tracks called "Scoring," "Checking," "Face Off" and "Power Play," Lafleur shared his hockey tips while singers and music played in the background. "I like disco," he said, "but I'm not a very good dancer."

The First Team Canada

These days, the name Team Canada is used for men's and women's teams competing for Canada in almost any international sport. The name was first used when NHL players from Canada played an eight-game series against the Soviet Union in September of 1972. That was the first time NHL players were allowed to represent Canada in international hockey. From 1963 until 1970, Canada was represented by a team of mostly university players known as the Canadian National Team, or the Nats for short. Before that, from 1920 until 1962, local teams — often the winner of the Allan Cup as Canada's amateur champion — played for their country in the Olympics or at the World Ice Hockey Championships.

NAME GAME:
Team Names

Here are the stories behind the names of some of the club teams that won early gold medals for Canada in international hockey . . .

Winnipeg Falcons
1920 Olympics

This team was made up mainly of members of the local Icelandic community in Winnipeg. The falcon is a symbol for Iceland much like the beaver is for Canada.

Trail Smoke Eaters
1939 and 1961 World Championships

Trail, British Columbia, is a mining town dating back to 1896. Some stories say the name Smoke Eaters comes from the many smokestacks of the local mine that towered over the city.

RCAF Flyers
1948 Olympics

The Flyers were a team organized by the Royal Canadian Air Force in 1947 to represent Canada at the 1948 Winter Olympics. The team consisted mainly of airmen, some of whom had served during World War II.

Edmonton Mercurys
1950 World Championships, 1952 Olympics
Formed in Edmonton in 1949, the team was named
for a Mercury automobile dealership that sponsored
them.

Penticton Vees
1955 World Championships
Penticton is a city in the Okanagan Valley of British
Columbia, an area known for its fruit growing. The
Vees were named for three popular varieties of
peaches grown there: the Victory, the Valiant and
the Vidette.

Playing Their Song

On January 7, 2019, Alexander Steen, Joel Edmundson, Robert Bortuzzo, Jaden Schwartz and Robby Fabbri of the St. Louis Blues were watching an NFL playoff game at a sports bar. During commercials, the DJ played "Gloria," a song by Laura Branigan that came out in 1982. The Blues players noticed how much fun everyone in the place was having whenever the song came on. So they decided "Gloria" should become the Blues' new theme song. They started playing "Gloria" in the dressing room after every win . . . and the wins kept on coming! When the Blues beat Dallas to win game seven of the Western Conference semifinal, St. Louis radio station Y98 played "Gloria" for 24 hours straight to celebrate. The station did it again two weeks later when the Blues advanced to the Stanley Cup Final. When the Blues beat Boston to win the Stanley Cup, fans all over St. Louis were celebrating to the strains of "Gloria"!

MASCOT MAYHEM

Louie is a polar bear with light blue fur who is the mascot for the St. Louis Blues. He wears a team jersey with the number 00 and his name on the back. Sometimes people refer to Louie as "Victory Dog" because it's not super obvious that he's a polar bear!

Rookie Record

Goalie Jordan Binnington was a huge reason why St. Louis won the Stanley Cup in 2019. Binnington was drafted by the Blues in 2011. Except for filling in for 13 minutes in one game with the Blues on January 14, 2016, he spent seven and a half years in the minor leagues before finally getting a chance with St. Louis in December of 2018. Binnington went 16-3-1 in his first 20 starts. He finished the season with a 24-5-1 record and a 1.89 goals-against average. Then, in the playoffs, Binnington led the Blues to the team's first Stanley Cup title by setting a rookie goalie record with 16 wins in the playoffs.

Winning Streak

Having a great goalie in net is a big help in the playoffs. In 1988 Grant Fuhr of the Edmonton Oilers was the first to have 4 wins in each of the 4 rounds for a total of 16 wins. Among the other goalies to have hit that mark, Patrick Roy (1993, 1996, 2001) and Martin Brodeur (1995, 2000, 2003) both did it three times.

With an extra round added to the playoffs in 2020, there was a chance for a goalie to break the 16-win record — and Andrei Vasilevskiy did it. The Tampa Bay star played all 25 games for the Lightning during the playoffs that year and won 18 of them. He ended the 2020 playoffs with a 2–0 shutout over the Dallas Stars to win the Stanley Cup.

Vasilevskiy was hot again throughout the playoffs in 2021. That year, he became the first goalie since Ken Dryden, with the Montreal Canadiens in 1977 and 1978, to win back-to-back championships while playing every game in the playoffs for his team.

Hartbreaker

Facing the Montreal Canadiens in the 2020 playoffs, Philadelphia's Carter Hart had two straight shutouts over three days. At 22 years and 5 days old, that made Hart the second-youngest goalie in NHL history to post back-to-back playoff shutouts. Detroit Red Wings rookie Harry Lumley was just 18 years and 161 days old when he had back-to-back shutouts during the Stanley Cup Final in 1945.

Did You Know?

Harry Lumley made his NHL debut with Detroit on December 19, 1943. It was just six weeks past his 17th birthday, making him the youngest goalie in NHL history. Several teenage players got their start in the NHL in the early 1940s because many older players in the league were serving in the armed forces during World War II.

BY THE NUMBERS

These are the youngest goalies ever to post a shutout in a regular-season NHL game:

PLAYER/AGE	SHUTOUT DATE	FINAL SCORE
Harry Lumley 18 years, 64 days	January 14, 1945	DET 3 – TOR 0
Tom Barrasso 18 years, 293 days	January 18, 1984	BUF 4 – LAK 0
Marc-Andre Fleury 18 years, 336 days	October 30, 2003	PIT 1 – CHI 0
Dan Blackburn 19 years, 171 days	November 7, 2002	NYR 1 – CGY 0
Bill Ranford 19 years, 316 days	October 26, 1986	BOS 6 – CGY 0

Worst Road Trip Ever

The Dawson City Klondikers, also known as the Nuggets, travelled more than 6,000 kilometres (4,000 mi.) to challenge the Ottawa Silver Seven for the 1905 Stanley Cup. The Klondikers left on December 18, 1904, expecting it to take them 18 days to reach Ottawa . . . but it took almost a week longer!

They journeyed by bicycle and on foot, by train and by boat — but not by dog sled, as sometimes reported — just to reach Vancouver. From there, they boarded a train to the capital, arriving on January 11, 1905. A little worse for wear, they were swept in their best-of-three Stanley Cup series.

ID Please

Even though his team gave up 32 goals in the two games played, everyone seemed to agree that Dawson City goalie Albert Forrest had played great. If not for him, many newspapers said, the score would have been even more one-sided. Many of those newspapers reported that Forrest was only 17 years old. For years he was thought to have been the youngest goalie ever to play in a Stanley Cup game. But official documents show that Forrest was born in Trois-Rivieres, Quebec, on January 11, 1886, making him 19 years old during the series and not the youngest goalie.

Aye Aye, Captain!

Currently, the longest-serving captain in the NHL is Sidney Crosby, who has worn the "C" in Pittsburgh since the 2007–08 season. Jonathan Toews became the captain of the Chicago Blackhawks in 2008–09, and Alex Ovechkin was given the "C" with the Washington Capitals in 2009–10.

But all three are going to have to stick around a while if they want to catch Steve Yzerman. Before he became the general manager of the Detroit Red Wings, Yzerman served as that team's captain for 20 years, from 1986 to 2006. He was actually the captain for 19 seasons because the 2004–05 campaign was wiped out by a lockout.

Cech Him Out

Growing up in the Czech Republic (when it was Czechoslovakia), Petr Cech played soccer and hockey. When he had to choose one sport over the other, he went with soccer . . . but he never lost his love for hockey!

Cech is considered to be one of the greatest goalies in the history of English Premier League football — the sport that we call soccer in North America. He began his pro soccer career in his home country at the age of 17 and was a star by the time he was 19. He later played with English Premier League teams Chelsea and Arsenal for 15 years and currently has a coaching role with Chelsea.

But after retiring as a soccer player in 2019, Cech took off his cleats and tied on his skates. He signed as a goalie with the Guildford Phoenix in a lower-level British hockey league.

When Cech returned to hockey at the age of 37, he chose to wear number 39 in honour of the great Czech goalie Dominik Hasek.

Big Zee on D

On February 24, 2022, Zdeno Chara broke the NHL record for most games played by a defenceman. The previous record was held by Chris Chelios, who played 1,651 games with four different teams over 26 seasons between 1983 and 2010. Chara, who played his first NHL game with the New York Islanders against the Detroit Red Wings on November 19, 1997, played game number 1,652 for the Islanders against the San Jose Sharks.

By the end of the 2021–22 season, only six players in NHL history had played more games than Chara, including Patrick Marleau (1,779), Gordie Howe (1,767), Mark Messier (1,756), Jaromir Jagr (1,733) and Ron Francis (1,731). Joe Thornton, who played with the Florida Panthers during the 2021–22 season, is the only active NHL player with more games than Chara. Thornton played in his 1,700th game on January 6, 2022.

Chara celebrated his 45th birthday on March 18, 2022. This makes him one of the oldest players in NHL history, along with Jaromir Jagr, Johnny Bower and Moe Roberts, who also played until they were that age. Only Gordie Howe (52) and Chris Chelios (48) played until they were older.

Did You Know?

Standing 2.06 metres (6 ft., 9 in.) tall, Zdeno Chara is the tallest player in NHL history.

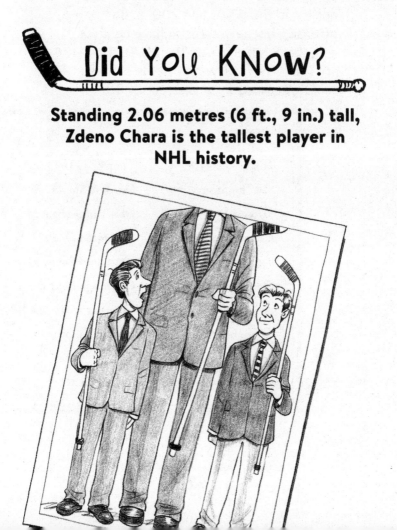

BY THE NUMBERS

New NHL teams and an emphasis on defensive hockey saw a scoring decline in the 1990s and 2000s. But offensive hockey seems to have begun a comeback heading into the 2020s. Here are the 10 NHL players with the highest-scoring seasons since the year 2000:

PLAYER	TEAM
Nikita Kucherov	Tampa Bay Lightning
Joe Thornton	San Jose Sharks
Jaromir Jagr	New York Rangers
Connor McDavid	Edmonton Oilers
Jaromir Jagr	Pittsburgh Penguins
Sidney Crosby	Pittsburgh Penguins
Joe Sakic	Colorado Avalanche
Connor McDavid	Edmonton Oilers
Johnny Gaudreau	Calgary Flames
Jonathan Huberdeau	Florida Panthers

POINTS (GOALS, ASSISTS)	SEASON
128 points (41G, 87A)	2018–19
125 points (29G, 96A)	2005–06
123 points (54G, 69A)	2005–06
123 points (44G, 79A)	2021–22
121 points (52G, 69A)	2000–01
120 points (36G, 84A)	2006–07
118 points (54G, 64A)	2000–01
116 points (41G, 75A)	2018–19
115 points (40G, 75A)	2021–22
115 points (30G, 85A)	2021–22

Carry a Big Stick

The world's largest hockey stick was built for the Canada Pavilion at the Expo 86 World's Fair in Vancouver. It's 62.5 metres (205 ft.) long and weighs 28 tonnes (62,000 lb.). The shaft and blade of the stick were made in sections with steel-reinforced Douglas fir beams measuring 90 centimetres by 120 centimetres (3 ft. by 4 ft.). The huge stick was trucked to Vancouver in two pieces, assembled, and then lifted into place on August 21, 1985, where it stood upright for two years.

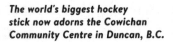

The world's biggest hockey stick now adorns the Cowichan Community Centre in Duncan, B.C.

NAME GAME:
Modern Edition

Justin Williams played 19 seasons in the NHL with four different teams between 2000 and 2020. He won the Stanley Cup once with Carolina in 2006 and twice with Los Angeles, in 2012 and 2014. Williams was known as "Mr. Game 7" for his big performances in the playoffs when it counted the most. His teams had a record of 8–1 in the nine game sevens that Williams played, and he had 7 goals and 8 assists for 15 points. Williams scored the Cup-clinching goal when the Hurricanes beat the Edmonton Oilers 3–1 in game seven in 2006. He won the Conn Smythe Trophy as playoff MVP in 2014 and had two goals and three assists in three game sevens during the Kings' championship run that year.

MASCOT MAYHEM

The official mascot of the Carolina Hurricanes is Stormy the Ice Pig. They chose a pig because the state of North Carolina has many hog farms. In fact, one of the men responsible for moving the team from Hartford, Connecticut, to North Carolina in 1997 wanted to call the team the Ice Hogs. Stormy has been the team's mascot since their first season and wears number 97.

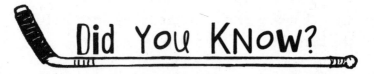

Did You Know?

On April 6, 1980, a then 52-year-old Gordie Howe played his 1,767th and final NHL game. He scored his 801st goal and 1,049th assist, helping the Hartford Whalers to a 5–3 win over the Detroit Red Wings. The 1979–80 season was Howe's last — and the Whalers' first. In 1997, the Whalers relocated to North Carolina, becoming the Carolina Hurricanes.

Parlez-Vous Français?

The Montreal Canadiens chose Cole Caufield with the 15th pick in the 2019 NHL Draft. Caufield grew up in Wisconsin, in the U.S. It's common for American high school students to study Spanish, but Cole studied French just in case he got drafted by Montreal! After spending two seasons with the University of Wisconsin, and winning the 2021 Hobey Baker Award as the top U.S. college hockey player, Caufield joined the Canadiens late in the 2020–21 season. He scored four goals in just 10 games played and then had 12 points in 20 playoff games to help Montreal reach the Stanley Cup Final. *Bien joué!*

BY THE NUMBERS

There have been 14 players in NHL history to score a hat trick on their birthday. One of them did it twice.

PLAYER	TEAM
Phil Esposito	Boston Bruins
Butch Goring	Los Angeles Kings
Gilbert Perreault	Buffalo Sabres
Mats Hallin	New York Islanders
Lanny McDonald	Calgary Flames
Mike Gartner	Washington Capitals
Wayne Gretzky	Edmonton Oilers
Paul MacLean	Winnipeg Jets
Jari Kurri	Edmonton Oilers
Wayne Gretzky	Los Angeles Kings
Dino Ciccarelli	Washington Capitals
Pavol Dimitra	St. Louis Blues
Patrick Sharp	Chicago Blackhawks
Viktor Arvidsson	Nashville Predators
Pavel Buchnevich	New York Rangers

DATE	FINAL SCORE
February 20, 1974 (age 32)	5–5 tie with Minnesota
October 22, 1975 (age 26)	5–3 win over Chicago
November 13, 1983 (age 33)	11–2 win over Calgary
March 19, 1983 (age 25)	9–2 win over Philadelphia
February 16, 1984 (age 31)	10–3 win over Pittsburgh
October, 29, 1985 (age 26)	6–3 win over St. Louis
January 26, 1985 (age 24)	6–3 win over Pittsburgh
March 9, 1988 (age 30)	6–6 tie with Calgary
May 18, 1990 (age 30)	7–2 win over Boston
January 26, 1991 (age 30)	5–4 win over Vancouver
February 8, 1991 (age 31)	6–3 win over Edmonton
November 29, 2002 (age 28)	7–2 win over Calgary
December 27, 2013 (age 32)	7–2 win over Colorado
April 8, 2021 (age 28)	7–1 win over Detroit
April 17, 2021 (age 26)	6–3 win over New Jersey

Great Scott!

John Scott was nobody's idea of an NHL superstar. He played on seven different teams in his eight seasons in the league. In that time, he played in 286 games. He had just five goals and six assists. At 2.03 metres (6 ft., 8 in.), and 118 kilograms (260 lb.), everybody knew Scott was there to add toughness to his teams.

In 2016 the NHL announced a new three-on-three tournament format for the All-Star Game. The change would showcase the speed and skill of NHL players. A couple of Toronto podcasters joked that it would be fun to see an underdog like John Scott play in the game, and it went viral on the internet. When the results of the All-Star voting were announced, Scott had received more votes than any other player in the NHL! He would be the captain of the Pacific team.

The league tried to convince Scott to drop out. Arizona even traded him to Montreal, who sent him to their minor-league team in St. John's, Newfoundland. But Scott played in the All-Star Game and his team won the tournament! He was named the MVP and got a new car as well as a share of the prize money.

In the end, everyone had a lot of fun with the story, except maybe the NHL. They passed a new rule for the 2017 All-Star Game. The "John Scott rule" says that players who are injured or in the minors can't be on the ballot and that if someone is voted captain and is hurt or playing in the minors, the player with the second-most votes gets in instead.

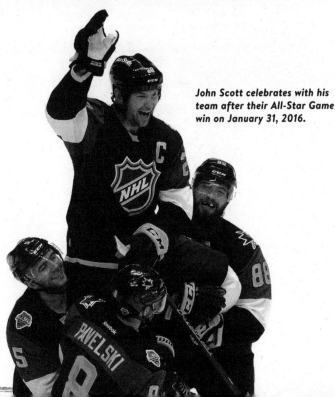

John Scott celebrates with his team after their All-Star Game win on January 31, 2016.

Trophy Tales

Right-winger Mathieu Joseph was born in
Laval (just north of Montreal) and grew up
in Montreal-Nord. After winning his second
Stanley Cup with the Lightning in 2021, he
knew just how to celebrate his day with
the Cup. He filled it with french fries, gravy
and cheese curds and chowed down on the
ultimate plate of poutine!

Oh, Brother!

When an injury prevented Auston Matthews from playing in the 2020 NHL All-Star Game, Brady Tkachuk of the Ottawa Senators was named to take his place. Brady's brother, Matthew Tkachuk of the Calgary Flames, had already been selected to play in the game. That made the Tkachuk brothers the first sibling combination to play in the All-Star Game since former Vancouver Canucks stars Daniel and Henrik Sedin in 2011.

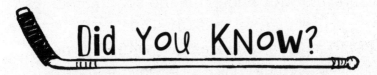

Did You Know?

Brothers Maurice Richard and Henri Richard played together in the All-Star Game four times in the 1950s.

The John Tavareses

John Tavares has had a stellar career. In minor hockey he was a standout for the Toronto Marlboros, and when he was just 14 years old, he was granted Exceptional Player Status by the Ontario Hockey League. This allowed Tavares to enter the OHL Draft in 2005 — a year early — where he was selected first overall by the Oshawa Generals. In the OHL, Tavares won the award for Rookie of the Year, going on to set a new league record with 215 goals over his four years there.

He was then selected first overall by the New York Islanders in the 2009 NHL Entry Draft, and was among the top-scoring rookies in his first year. In the 2011–12 season, Tavares played all 82 games, with 31 goals, 50 assists and 81 points. He was the fourth Islander to score at least 73 points in a season at age 21 or younger, joining Hall of Famers Mike Bossy, Bryan Trottier and Denis Potvin. It was little surprise when he was named captain before the 2013–14 season.

On July 1, 2018, Tavares signed with the team he had cheered for as a boy: the Toronto Maple Leafs. Tavares set career highs of 47 goals and 88 points with Toronto during the 2018–19 season and was named captain the next year. But good as he is, John Tavares might be only the second-best athlete named John Tavares in his own family!

John's uncle, also named John Tavares, is the leading scorer in the history of the National Lacrosse League. In 24 seasons with the Buffalo Bandits, from 1992 to 2015, Tavares set NLL records for games played and assists, and still holds the all-time record for goals (815) and points (1749). He also spent 30 seasons playing with several teams in the Canadian Lacrosse Association. From 1983 to 2012, Tavares won eight league scoring titles and seven Mann Cup Championships. He's pretty much the Wayne Gretzky of lacrosse. That's a lot for his nephew to live up to!

NAME GAME: Classic Edition

Rick Vaive played with four NHL teams from 1979 until 1992. His best years were in Toronto. Vaive was the first Maple Leaf to hit 50 goals in a season, scoring 54 in 1981–82 and repeating that success in the next two seasons. He also served as captain from 1982 until 1986.

Vaive was born in Ottawa but moved to Prince Edward Island when he was 11. Years later, when Vaive turned pro with the WHA's Birmingham Bulls, he earned the nickname "Spud" because PEI is known for its potatoes. One day at practice, Coach John Brophy started yelling "Squid!" Teammate Craig Hartsburg asked who he was calling for.

"Vaive," said Brophy.

"Oh, you mean Spud."

"Spud, Squid . . . I don't [care] what you call him. Get him down here!"

Years later, in a Leafs game against the Minnesota North Stars, Vaive and Hartsburg ran into each other. Hartsburg greeted his old friend with "Hey, Squid, how's it going?" One of the other Leafs heard it and thought it was hilarious. From that day on, Vaive became "Squid."

Off–Ice Superstar, Team USA

Kendall Coyne Schofield has been a member of the U.S. National Women's Team since 2011, winning eight World Championship medals (six gold, two silver) and three Olympic medals (one gold, two silver). She has appeared in two NHL Skills Competitions: the 2019 Fastest Skater event and again in 2020 when Canadian and American women's teams played in a 20-minute three-on-three game.

She has also worked as a colour commentator on San Jose Sharks broadcasts and was hired by the Chicago Blackhawks in 2020 as a player development coach for their top minor-league team.

Off-Ice Superstar, Team Canada

Hayley Wickenheiser is the greatest player in the history of women's hockey, playing 23 years with the Canadian National Women's Team. When she retired in 2017, she finished her medical degree and became a doctor. Since 2018, she's also worked in the front office of the Toronto Maple Leafs and in 2021 she was appointed senior director of player development. In early 2020, Dr. Wickenheiser joined forces with Conquer COVID-19, a volunteer-led organization that collected three million pieces of personal protective equipment for vulnerable frontline workers.

Did You Know?

Hayley Wickenheiser is the first woman to score a goal in a professional men's hockey league. She played with the Finnish men's team HCK Salamat.

Lost Leagues

When the Canadian Women's Hockey League collapsed in the spring of 2019, it left the U.S.-based National Women's Hockey League as the only pro league for top female players. Formed in 2015, the NWHL added its first Canadian team for the 2020–21 season with the creation of the Toronto Six. The NWHL was reorganized as the Premier Hockey Federation for the 2021–22 season.

Going to the Dogs

The Dallas Stars may be the only NHL team with a pet cow, but plenty of teams have pet dogs. Two of the newest pups joined the league for the 2021–22 season. The Washington Capitals partnered with a non-profit group that trains service dogs for war veterans. Biscuit joined the Capitals on the first day of training camp in September of 2021, when the chocolate Lab was nine weeks old. Biscuit worked with the front office staff and made appearances at special events, practices and some home games. Being in many different situations helps future service dogs learn to be calm and dependable.

Around the same time that Biscuit joined the Capitals, the Edmonton Oilers signed Flex to a two-year contract. Five months old at the time, Flex is a female Lab from the Dogs with Wings Assistance Dog Society in Edmonton. After two years with the team, Flex will find her "forever home" with a person who can benefit from her help.

Barclay was a service-dog-in-training with the St. Louis Blues from 2018 to 2021, then he became the first ambassador dog for a professional sports team. In his new role, Barclay helped show the positive impact of assistance dogs. The yellow Lab, who is named for former Blues star Barclay Plager, was nine months old when St. Louis won the Stanley Cup in the spring of 2019. The team crowned him the first ever "Stanley Pup Champion."

NAME GAME:
Modern Edition

David Pastrnak plays right wing for the
Boston Bruins, on the team's top line with
center Patrice Bergeron and left-winger Brad
Marchand. Together, the trio is known as "the
Perfection Line." Pastrnak is known by the
nickname "Pasta," and pasta is pretty much
all he eats on game days.

Hungry, Hungry Hockey

Shortly before the start of the 2021–22 season, David Pastrnak teamed up with a supermarket chain to announce a unique fundraiser. Stores in Massachusetts, Rhode Island and Connecticut sold Bruins-coloured black and gold boxes of penne pasta featuring an autographed picture of Pastrnak to raise money for pediatric cancer research. The boxes sold for just 88 cents to match his uniform number.

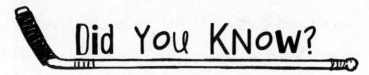

Did You Know?

Hockey stars have been making appearances in the cereal aisle for a long time. Limited-edition boxes of breakfast favourites have included March Munch, Fedorov Crunch, MacKinnon Krunch, Fleury Flakes, Oshie O's, Ovi O's and Hull-O's.

BY THE NUMBERS

Nine sets of teammates have skated together in more than 1,000 NHL games. The most recent are Alex Ovechkin and Nicklas Backstrom, who topped 1,000 games together with the Washington Capitals during the 2021–22 season. Dustin Brown and Anze Kopitar are also active players who have played more than 1,000 games together, with the Los Angeles Kings. The other seven sets of teammates are:

PLAYERS	TEAM(S)	GAMES
Gordie Howe & Alex Delvecchio	Detroit	1,353
Daniel Sedin & Henrik Sedin	Vancouver	1,276
Nicklas Lidstrom & Kris Draper	Detroit	1,107
Duncan Keith & Brent Seabrook	Chicago	1,069
Bob Gainey & Larry Robinson	Montreal	1,058
George Armstrong & Tim Horton	Toronto	1,026
Mark Messier & Kevin Lowe	Edmonton/ NY Rangers	1,007

Odds on Edwards

Only four players with the last name Edwards have ever played in the NHL. All four are goalies: Roy Edwards (1969–1974), Marv Edwards (1969–1974), Gary Edwards (1968–1982) and Don Edwards (1977–1986).

EBUG for the WIN!

David Ayres grew up in Whitby, Ontario, and got to Junior B as a goalie. He bounced around the lower minor leagues for a little bit, but his playing career ended around 2004 when he required a kidney transplant. Fortunately his mother was a match. Ayres stuck around hockey, though. He was a maintenance worker at Toronto's Mattamy Centre and also drove the Zamboni machine. Starting in 2012, he sometimes served as practice goalie for the Maple Leafs and the Toronto Marlies.

He dressed as an emergency backup goalie — or EBUG — with the Marlies twice, but never got into a game.

Then, on February 22, 2020, the Leafs played the Hurricanes in Toronto. Carolina's starting goalie, James Reimer, had faced only one shot in the game before being hurt at 3:07 of the first period. Then at 11:19 of the second period, Carolina's second goalie, Petr Mrazek, got hurt too. The call went out for the EBUG — Ayres would get his chance.

It was 3–1 Hurricanes when Ayres took to the ice against Toronto, and Carolina upped its lead to 4–1 less than two minutes later. Ayres let in the first two shots he faced but quickly settled in, stopping a big shot from Auston Matthews late in the second period.

The Hurricanes took their 4–3 lead into the third period, and because Ayres had been the goalie when Carolina scored its fourth goal, he now had a chance to win the game! Ayres stopped all seven shots he faced in the third period, and Carolina scored twice for a 6–3 victory. This made Ayres the first EBUG to win a game and, at age 42, the oldest goalie to win their NHL debut.

Ayres appeared on several TV shows over the next few days, then flew down to Raleigh, North Carolina, for the Hurricanes' home game against Dallas on Tuesday, February 25. The mayor of Raleigh declared it "David Ayres Day" in the city, and the Hurricanes sold special T-shirts with his number 90 on the back. Ayres gave some of the proceeds to a kidney foundation in the city.

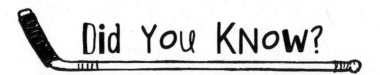

Did You Know?

The **EBUG** rule was designed so that no team would ever have to play without a real goalie on the ice. Teams dress only 2 goalies for a game, but they usually dress 6 or 7 defencemen and 12 or 13 forwards. That means if a forward or a defenceman gets hurt during a game, teams just have to juggle their lineup to cover off the missing player. No emergency substitutes for those positions are allowed since there are still plenty of players to fill the gap.

EREF?

If a referee or a linesman gets injured, there are rules for that too. The NHL has been using two referees and two linesmen in every game since the 2000–01 season. If one referee gets hurt and can't continue, the other will handle all of the responsibilities and the game goes on. If one of the linesmen has to leave a game, the two referees will help the one remaining linesman with their duties. In either case, if a spare referee or linesman happens to be there, they can be substituted in.

Things become trickier if a referee or a linesman can't start the game at all. According to NHL Rule 31.11 ". . . the League will make every attempt to find suitable replacement officials, otherwise, the Managers or Coaches of the two Clubs shall agree on Referee(s) and Linesman(men). If they are unable to agree, they shall appoint a player from each side who shall act as Referee and Linesman; the player of the home Club acting as Referee and the player of the visiting Club as Linesman."

EREFs in Action

On January 15, 1983, the New Jersey Devils were scheduled to visit the Hartford Whalers. On their way to the game, referee Ron Fournier (there was only one referee used in those days) and linesman Dan Marouelli got stuck in a snowstorm. When the teams were ready to start the game, only linesman Ron Foyt was there. Foyt took over the referee duties. Hartford chose defenceman Mickey Volcan to be a replacement linesman. He had hurt his hand in the team's morning skate and wasn't going to be able to play. Garry Howatt from New Jersey hadn't been in the lineup for a couple of weeks because of his own injury, so the Devils chose him to be the other linesman.

Volcan and Howatt worked the first period, handling a few faceoffs and calling some offsides. They also got between players during a shouting match with Hartford's Ed Hospodar and New Jersey's Mike Antonovich. What would have happened if a real fight had broken out? "We were each supposed to grab our own player if something started," Volcan later told reporters. Fournier and Marouelli showed up in time for the second period.

It wasn't just the referee and linesman who had trouble with the snow that night. Only 4,812 fans braved the storm to attend the game. Those who made it were allowed to sit in the best seats, and they went home happy after the Whalers scored in the third period to give them a 2–1 victory.

Rulebook Ridiculousness

During an April 13, 2008 game, New York Rangers forward Sean Avery hung around the front of New Jersey Devils goalie Martin Brodeur, waving his stick in the netminder's face and obstructing his view by standing right in front of him. The next day, the NHL created the Sean Avery rule, giving a two-minute penalty to any player who does this.

Lefty Is All Right

Before the NHL required teams to carry two goalies, starting in 1965–66, it was more common to see an emergency goalie in the net. If it was only for a short time, another position player on the team would take over. For longer stretches, they'd often bring in a local junior player. Sometimes it was the home team's trainer.

Ross Wilson — better known as Lefty Wilson — was the trainer for the Detroit Red Wings from 1950 until 1982. He'd been a goalie growing up in Toronto and played a few years of pro hockey in the Red Wings' minor leagues. During the 1950s, he played three games in the NHL as an emergency goalie.

On October 10, 1953, Wilson suited up for the Red Wings to cover for an injured Terry Sawchuk in a losing effort against Montreal. On January 22, 1956, he replaced Harry Lumley for the Toronto Maple Leafs during a 4–1 Detroit victory. Both times, he didn't allow a single goal. Then on December 29, 1957,

Wilson suited up for the Boston Bruins against the Red Wings, replacing an injured Don Simmons in a game that ended in a 2–2 tie. Wilson let in one goal in that game.

Lefty Wilson is the only goalie in NHL history who played three career games with three different teams. He saw a total of 80 minutes and 44 seconds of action and allowed just one goal, for a goals-against average of 0.74. Records are incomplete for his first game, but in the last two he stopped 32 of the 33 shots he faced. Not bad at all!

Did You Know?

One of the Original Six NHL teams, the Red Wings were founded in 1926. They were known as the Cougars until 1930. For the next two seasons they were called the Falcons but changed their name again, to the Red Wings, in 1932.

MASCOT MAYHEM

Al the Octopus has been the mascot of the Detroit Red Wings since 1995. There's no one wearing a costume though. This mascot is a large purple prop in a Red Wings jersey that is raised and lowered from the rafters above the arena in Detroit. But why an octopus?

During the 1952 Stanley Cup final two Detroit fans threw a real octopus onto the ice for luck, to represent the eight games a team then needed to win the Cup. The Red Wings won the game and the tradition of throwing an octopus on the ice began. Al is named after Al Sobotka, who was the long-time arena maintenance manager. He often had the slippery job of picking up the octopuses that were thrown on the ice.

Staal Together

On March 12, 2022, Marc Staal of the Detroit Red Wings played the 1,000th game of his NHL career. He became the third member of the Staal family, along with his brothers Eric and Jordan, to reach the 1,000-game milestone. A fourth brother, Jared Staal, also played in the NHL, but he played only two games with the Carolina Hurricanes late in the 2012–13 season. In his NHL debut on April 25, 2013, Jared started the game on a line with Eric and Jordan. The game was against the New York Rangers, which was Marc Staal's team at the time, but Marc was out with an injury.

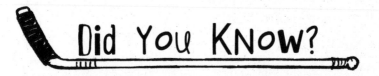

Did You Know?

Marc Staal is the second oldest of the brothers, but his younger brother Jordan Staal played in the NHL a year before him. Jordan made his NHL debut on October 5, 2006, and Marc made his on October 4, 2007.

Bye-Bye to the Best

In 2020–21, at age 36, Marc-Andre Fleury won the Vezina Trophy as the NHL's best goalie for the first time in his career. But it wasn't enough to keep him in Vegas. Facing a tight budget, the Golden Knights traded Fleury to the Chicago Blackhawks shortly after the season ended. Then, near the end of the 2021-22 season, Chicago traded him to the Minnesota Wild. It may seem strange to get rid of the NHL's best goalie, but it wasn't the first time.

Lorne Chabot won the Vezina with the Chicago Black Hawks in 1934–35. He hurt his knee in training camp before the next season and then refused to report to the minor leagues. Chicago later traded him to the Montreal Canadiens, who then traded him to the Montreal Maroons. Some people consider Chabot to be the greatest goalie never elected to the Hockey Hall of Fame.

When Terry Sawchuk earned the Vezina with Detroit in 1954–55, it was the third time he'd won the trophy in four seasons. Still, with another star goalie, Glenn Hall, waiting in the minors, the Red Wings traded Sawchuk to the Boston Bruins after the season. Sawchuk continued to star in the NHL until 1970, winning the Vezina again with Toronto in 1965, and is considered one of the greatest goalies of all time.

After joining the Black Hawks in 1957, Glenn Hall won the Vezina Trophy twice, in 1962–63 and in 1966–67. Even so, they made him available in the NHL Expansion Draft in June of 1967, and he was selected by the St. Louis Blues. Hall won the Vezina again in 1969 and was elected to the Hockey Hall of Fame in 1975.

Michel Larocque was dealt to the Toronto Maple Leafs by the Montreal Canadiens midway through a Vezina Trophy–winning season in 1980–81. He was mainly a backup goalie throughout his career in Toronto and Montreal.

Jim Carey won the Vezina Trophy with Washington in 1995–96, but he got traded to Boston midway through the 1996–97 season.

Carey had been a big star with the Capitals, but was out of hockey by 1999.

Dominik Hasek won the Vezina Trophy for the sixth time in his nine seasons with Buffalo in 2000–01, but the cash-strapped Sabres could no longer afford him, so they traded him to Detroit. Hasek won the Stanley Cup with the Red Wings in 2002 and 2008 and made the Hall of Fame in 2014.

NAME GAME:
Modern Edition

Marc-Andre Fleury is known as Flower, from the English translation of his French last name. Hockey Hall of Famer Guy Lafleur was often called the Flower for the same reason.

BY THE NUMBERS

When he made the playoffs with Vegas in 2021, Marc-Andre Fleury became the first goalie in NHL history to play in the post-season 15 years in a row. Tony Esposito held the old record of 14 straight seasons in the playoffs, from 1970 through 1983. Fleury made the playoffs for the 16th time with Minnesota in 2022. The only goalies in NHL history to make the playoffs that many times are:

GOALIE	PLAYOFF APPEARANCES
Martin Brodeur	17 times in 22 seasons
Patrick Roy	17 times in 19 seasons
Marc-Andre Fleury	16 times in 16 seasons
Andy Moog	16 times in 18 seasons
Jacques Plante	16 times in 18 seasons

OHL Inroads

On June 5, 2021, the Sarnia Sting used their pick in the 14th round of the 2021 Ontario Hockey League Draft to select Taya Currie. The 16-year-old goalie from the Elgin-Middlesex Chiefs became the first female player to be drafted by an OHL team. She'd been playing with boys' teams since she was 10 years old, and was just the second girl in Ontario ever to play at the province's under-16 AAA level.

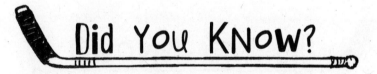

Did You Know?

Four female goalies have played major junior hockey in the CHL. Manon Rheaume played with the Trois-Rivieres Draveurs in the QMJHL in 1991, while Charline Labonte played for the Acadie-Bathurst Titan from 1999 to 2001. Shannon Szabados played for the Tri-City Americans of the WHL in 2002. Eve Gascon played with the Gatineau Olympiques in the QMJHL during the 2021-22 season.

Lots of Languages

In addition to the regular Saturday night TV broadcasts in English, French and Punjabi, on April 24, 2021, two NHL games were streamed online in seven of Canada's most commonly spoken languages. An early broadcast of Toronto versus Vancouver and a late broadcast of Edmonton versus Winnipeg were aired in Cantonese, Mandarin, Hindi, Vietnamese, Tagalog, German and Arabic.

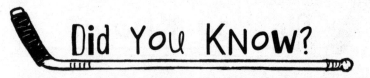

Did You Know?

Sportsnet and APTN debuted *Hockey Night in Canada in Cree* starting March 5, 2022. The weekly Saturday-night show features a game with Canadian NHL teams, with play-by-play by Clarence Iron and host Earl Wood. The now-weekly program built on the success of the first national television broadcast of an NHL game in the Plains Cree language on March 24, 2019.

Spelling It Right

In an exhibition game between Edmonton and Calgary on July 28, 2020, Oilers defenceman Ethan Bear wore a jersey with his usual number 74, but with his name spelled using Cree syllabics.

"It's very honourable to the players that played before me and then to the young Indigenous kids who want to play in the NHL. It's very honourable for me," said Bear after the game. "I wore it with pride tonight. It was very awesome."

Ethan Bear warming up before the exhibition game against the Calgary Flames. The Oilers bested the Flames 4–1.

Not Just a Jersey

In January of 2020, the Winnipeg Jets
and their farm club, the Manitoba Moose,
introduced jerseys with logos designed by
graphic design student Leticia Spence, of
Pimicikamak Cree Nation. The logos featured
elements of Indigenous cultures including
medicine wheels and floral motifs. The jerseys
were part of the second annual Winnipeg
Aboriginal Sport Achievement Centre (WASAC)
Night hosted by the Jets, and Follow Your
Dreams Day, hosted by the Moose. Jets players
wore their jerseys in the pre-game skate before
their game with the Tampa Bay Lightning
on January 17, 2020. The jerseys were then
auctioned off to raise money for WASAC.
The specialty jerseys were such a hit that
the Jets and the Moose carried on with the
program and now offer hats, t-shirts, pucks,
pins and hoodies featuring the logo on their
website.

Family Footsteps

Leah Hextall's grandfather, Bryan Hextall, starred with the New York Rangers in the 1940s. Her uncles, Bryan Jr. and Dennis Hextall, played in the NHL between 1963 and 1980. Her cousin, Ron Hextall, was a star goalie in the 1980s and 1990s and is currently the general manager of the Pittsburgh Penguins.

Leah also loved hockey but she knew that she wasn't quite good enough as a player. Instead, she pursued a career in broadcasting. After working in television since 2005, Leah Hextall became the first woman to do the play-by-play on a nationally televised NHL broadcast when she called a game between the Vegas Golden Knights and the Calgary Flames for Sportsnet on March 8, 2020. Hextall was part of an all-female lineup — including the broadcast team and the production crew — as the NHL helped to celebrate International Women's Day. Hextall was hired by ESPN as a reporter and to call play-by-play for the 2021–22 season.

NAME GAME:
Modern Edition

Selected seventh overall by Buffalo in 2019, Dylan Cozens is the first player from Yukon to be chosen in the first round of the NHL Draft. He debuted with the Sabres on January 14, 2021, and already has two pretty cool nicknames. He's known as "the Workhorse from Whitehorse" and "the Yukon Goal Rush."

"The Workhorse" is not to be confused with "the Powerhorse," Josh Anderson's nickname. The Montreal Canadiens forward is known for his speed and physicality.

BY THE NUMBERS

Quinn Hughes of the Vancouver Canucks led all NHL rookies in scoring during the 2019–20 season. It was a pretty rare feat for a defenceman. Hughes joined Hall of Famers Bobby Orr and Brian Leetch as the only blueliners to top the rookie scoring parade.

PLAYER	ROOKIE SEASON	TEAM	POINTS (GOALS ASSISTS)
Quinn Hughes	2019–20	Vancouver Canucks	53 points (8G, 45A)
Brian Leetch	1988–89	New York Rangers	71 points (23G, 48A)
Bobby Orr	1966–67	Boston Bruins	41 points (13G, 28A)

Jurassic Mark

Just prior to the 2021–22 season, the Seattle Kraken announced that Mark Giordano would be their first captain, but he didn't stick around for long. On March 20, 2022, Giordano was traded to the Toronto Maple Leafs. Before he was selected by Seattle in the NHL Expansion Draft, Giordano had spent the first 15 seasons of his NHL career with the Calgary Flames. He had been the captain in Calgary for eight of those years. Giordano had perhaps his best season with the Flames in 2018–19. That year, he joined Hall of Famers Ray Bourque, Nicklas Lidstrom and Sergei Zubov as the only defencemen in NHL history to score more than 70 points at the age of 35 or older. He became the first Flames player to win the Norris Trophy as the league's best defenceman and was also just the fourth player to win the award at age 35 or older, joining Lidstrom and two other Hall of Famers, Al MacInnis and Doug Harvey.

Philadelphia Didn't Fly

The 2021–22 season was a struggle for the Philadelphia Flyers. During the early part of the season, the Flyers became the first team in NHL history to suffer two different 10-game losing streaks in the first 40 games of their schedule. The Flyers lost 10 in a row from November 18 through December 8, 2021. Then, from December 30, 2021 until January 25, 2022, Philadelphia lost 13 straight games, which set a Flyers franchise record for the longest losing streak in team history.

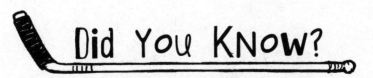

Did You Know?

The Pittsburgh Penguins hold the record for the longest winning streak in NHL history at 17 games, which was set in the 1992–93 season.

Sweep and Sour

The Winnipeg Jets scored a surprising sweep of the Edmonton Oilers in the first round of the 2021 NHL playoffs. In the second round, the Jets were the victims of an even more surprising sweep when they were beaten by the Montreal Canadiens. Winnipeg became just the fourth team in NHL history to open the playoffs with a four-game sweep, only to be knocked out in four straight games in their next series. The other teams are the 1992–93 Buffalo Sabres, the 2018–19 New York Islanders, and both the 1969–70 and 1971–72 Chicago Black Hawks.

Fun While It Lasted

The Arizona Coyotes missed the playoffs for seven straight seasons before reaching the post-season in 2019–20. They defeated the Nashville Predators three games to one to win the qualifying round, then faced the Colorado Avalanche in the first round. After three tight games, Arizona was blown out 7–1 in game four, then eliminated in game five when they lost by the same 7–1 score. Only once in NHL history has a team been knocked out of the playoffs by a combined two-game score higher than 14–2. In the semifinals in 1944, Montreal beat Toronto 4–1 in game four and 11–0 in game five for a total of 15–1.

Like Father, Like Son

Like his dad, Dale, Mason McTavish played junior hockey with the Pembroke Lumber Kings and the Peterborough Petes. When the OHL cancelled its 2020-21 season because of the COVID-19 pandemic, Mason played in Switzerland, where he was born while his dad was playing hockey there. The move paid off when the Anaheim Ducks chose Mason as the third overall pick in the 2021 NHL Draft.

Mason made the team in training camp before the 2021–22 season and was a surprise starter when the Ducks began the regular season on October 13, 2021. Father Dale had a long career in pro hockey, from 1995 until 2011, but he played only nine games in the NHL, for the Calgary Flames in 1996–97. Mason matched his father's NHL goal total of 1 in that first game against the Winnipeg Jets, a 4–1 Anaheim victory. At 18 years and 256 days old, Mason became the youngest player in Ducks history to score a goal.

Are We There Yet?

When the New York Islanders began their 2021–22 season, their brand new UBS Arena wasn't ready yet. So the NHL scheduled the Islanders to play 13 straight road games over 33 days, the longest road trip ever to start a season. It lasted from their first season game, October 14, until November 16, 2021. The Islanders and their fans alike were ecstatic to finally have an arena to call home on November 20, even if they did lose to the Flames 5–2. In fact, it took eight games for the Islanders to finally win their first game at the UBS Arena — the longest losing streak in a new venue.

Playing the Long Game

A group of 40 players in Alberta braved freezing temperatures to play the world's longest hockey game early in 2021. The two teams played 24 hours a day starting on February 4 and ending on February 15 for a total of 252 consecutive hours! Making things even harder was the fact that the community of Sherwood Park, near Edmonton, where the game was played, was in the middle of a deep freeze that saw temperatures plummet to a low of about -55°C during some of those days. The 2021 event was the seventh edition of the World's Longest Hockey Game, which is held to raise money for cancer research. When it started in 2003, 40 players played for "only" 80 straight hours. The 252-hour game raised $1.84 million, which brought the total raised since 2003 to $5.47 million. Team Hope captured the 2021 title by a score of 2,649 to 2,528 over Team Cure.

Did You Know?

The longest game in NHL history was a playoff game between the Detroit Red Wings and the Montreal Maroons. It started at 8:30 p.m. on the evening of March 24, 1936, and ended around 2:30 the next morning. Detroit won the game 1–0 at 16:30 of the sixth overtime period. That meant the teams played a total of 116 minutes and 30 seconds of overtime. When you add in the 60 minutes of regulation time, that comes to 176:30 of total playing time, or almost three complete games in one night. That's still the NHL record, but on March 12 and 13, 2017, two pro teams in Norway played a game that stretched until 17:46 of the eighth overtime period! That's a total of 217 minutes and 14 seconds of playing time. Players ate pizza and pasta between periods to keep their strength up.

BY THE NUMBERS

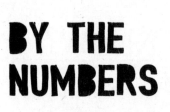

Alex Ovechkin is the eighth player in NHL history to score 700 goals. Having played his entire career with the Washington Capitals makes Ovi one of only two players to score 700 goals with the same team. Gordie Howe scored 786 of his 801 career goals for the Detroit Red Wings. These four players are the only others in NHL history to have scored as many as 600 goals for one team:

PLAYER, TEAM	GOALS	TOTAL NHL GOALS
Steve Yzerman, Detroit Red Wings	692 (1983 to 2006)	692
Mario Lemieux, Pittsburgh Penguins	690 (1984 to 2006)	690
Joe Sakic, Colorado Avalanche*	625 (1988 to 2009)	625
Bobby Hull, Chicago Black Hawks	604 (1957 to 1972)	610

Sakic played with the Quebec Nordiques from 1988 through 1995 before the franchise moved to Colorado.

Pee-Wee Power!

The Quebec International Pee-Wee Hockey Tournament was founded in 1960. It has gone on to become the most famous tournament in the world for young hockey players. Over the years, more than 1,200 future NHL or WHA players have taken part in the event. When the NHL published its list of 100 greatest players to mark the league's 100th birthday in 2017, 20 players on that list had played at the Pee-Wee Tournament.

The 1977 tournament alone featured five future Hockey Hall of Famers. Among them were Mario Lemieux, Pat LaFontaine, Patrick Roy and Steve Yzerman. The surprise winners that year were the Winnipeg Monarchs, led by another future Hall of Famer, Brett Hull.

Connor McDavid played at the Quebec International Pee-Wee Tournament in 2009. He represented the York-Simcoe Express of Aurora, Ontario, a minor hockey program not far from where he grew up in Newmarket. His coach was his father.

When Auston Matthews played at the Quebec tournament a year later, it involved a lot more travel. Matthews flew across the United States from his home in Scottsdale, Arizona, to a tryout in New Jersey for Druzhba-78 Kharkov . . . a pee-wee team from Ukraine! Matthews made the team and collected six points in three games for them in Quebec. "That was kind of my first time away from home," Matthews would later recall. "I was pretty nervous. That was my first time in front of a big crowd."

Did You Know?

On January 12, 2022, Auston Matthews set a franchise record for a road trip scoring streak, in a game against the Arizona Coyotes, with his 12th goal in 10 games. But he didn't quite catch the NHL record of 15 goals in 11 games, set by Pavel Bure in the 1993–94 season.

Not Those Maple Leafs!

There aren't a lot of kids living in Montreal's suburbs who would say the Toronto Maple Leafs are their favourite hockey team, but Jacob Bertrand loves them. For his eighth birthday in December of 2019, Jacob wanted a Leafs cake. When his family received the custom-made cake just before his party, it turned out to have the logo of Maple Leaf Foods by mistake! When Maple Leaf Foods found out about the error, they arranged to send Jacob and his family to Toronto to see the Leafs play against Edmonton on January 6, 2020. The Oilers beat the Leafs 6–4 that night, so Jacob didn't get to see his team win the game, but he did get a hockey stick signed by his favourite Maple Leafs players.

A Real Marn Burger

In honour of National Burger Day on May 28, 2020, restaurants across North America participated in a three-day burger showdown featuring burgers designed by celebrities. Included in the list of famous Canadian burger chefs was Mitch Marner of the Maple Leafs. Toronto was the only Canadian city included in the challenge but Mitch's burger wasn't just voted the best in Toronto, it was one of the top five Best Overall Burgers from among all 10 cities that took part. His burger was actually pretty simple. It was a beef patty with ketchup, mayonnaise, bacon and cheese.

Auston Fast-thews

On October 25, 2021, Auston Matthews scored the 200th goal of his NHL career. Matthews reached the milestone in his 338th career game. How fast is that? Well, in the history of the NHL, only 18 players have scored 200 goals in fewer games than Matthews. Of players currently active in the NHL, only Alex Ovechkin needed fewer games to score 200. (Ovi reached the milestone in his 296th game back in 2008–09.) Matthews is the fastest U.S.-born player to reach the 200-goal mark, breaking Kevin Stevens's record of 363 games. He's the second-fastest player to reach the mark in the history of the Toronto Maple Leafs.

Back on December 16, 1937, Charlie Conacher scored his 200th career NHL goal in his 317th game. During his nine seasons with the Maple Leafs from 1929 through 1938, Conacher was the NHL's leading goal-scorer five times and he led the league in points twice.

200 x 3 =

In addition to Auston Matthews, two other NHL superstars reached the 200-goal plateau in the early days of the 2021–22 season. First was Leon Draisaitl of Edmonton, scoring his 200th goal in his 481st career game on October 19, 2021. Just two days later, teammate Connor McDavid scored his 200th goal in his 411th game. In Oilers history, only Hockey Hall of Famers Wayne Gretzky (242 games), Jari Kurri (328) and Glenn Anderson (348) reached 200 goals faster than McDavid did.

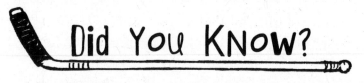

Did You Know?

Leon Draisaitl of the Edmonton Oilers was the first German player to be awarded the Art Ross Trophy as the NHL scoring leader, in 2019–20. That season he also won the Hart Trophy for Most Valuable Player and the Ted Lindsay Award for most outstanding player as chosen by fellow players, becoming the first player from Germany to win either of those too.

Two by Two by Two by Two

The 2021–22 season was not a very good one for the Montreal Canadiens. After reaching the Stanley Cup Finals in the spring of 2021, the Canadiens were the worst team in the NHL, finishing last in 32nd place overall.

On February 9, 2022, the Canadiens fired their coach, Dominique Ducharme. They replaced him with Martin St. Louis, who was a former NHL star but who had never coached beyond his own children's bantam and high school teams. When St. Louis got his first win as an NHL coach on February 17, 2022, it came against the St. Louis Blues. It was only Montreal's second win in 2022, and the victory (3–2 in overtime) came on two goals from Cole Caufield — who wears number 22. Caufield's second goal of the game was the game-winner. It was scored at 2:22 of overtime.

Read even MORE hockey trivia!

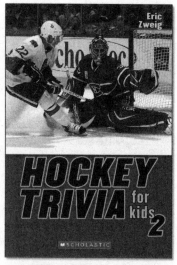

978-0-545-99699-0

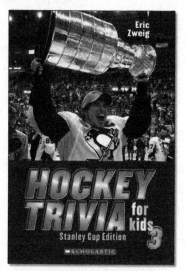

978-1-4431-0466-1

978-1-4431-4609-8

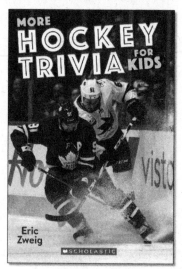

978-1-4431-4680-7